Management for Cannibals

Management for Cannibals

✦

How to Become Chief Eating Officer

Gaia and Ely Asher

iUniverse, Inc.
New York Lincoln Shanghai

Management for Cannibals
How to Become Chief Eating Officer

iUniverse, Inc.

For information address:
iUniverse
2021 Pine Lake Road, Suite 100
Lincoln, NE 68512
www.iuniverse.com

For question about rights and permissions contact:
Galiel.Net
704 228th Ave. NE, # 173
Sammamish, WA 98074-7222
http://www.Galiel.Net
Cannibal@Galiel.Net

ISBN: 0-595-28380-2 (Pbk)
ISBN: 0-595-65778-8 (Cloth)

'A slow sort of country!' said the Queen. 'Now, *here*, you see, it takes all the running *you* can do, to keep in the same place. If you want to get somewhere else, you must run at least twice as fast as that!'

"Through the Looking Glass"
Lewis Carroll

CONTENTS

PREFACE

This book is an attempt to reconstruct the art of management how it existed on a certain island of cannibal tribes during the past century. As such, we have to state that any similarity between the ideas in this book and the ideas expressed in books on corporate management are purely accidental.

Readers without a sense of humor are strongly advised against reading this book. Without the protective power of humor, the reality described in this book may be so shocking and repelling that it will induce an uncontrollable psychological rejection, resulting in blaming the authors for black-mouthing and mocking the island's corporate culture.

A.D. 2100

LIFE IN THE TRIBE

Be friendly, likable, and fun,
Respectful be to everyone:
To boss, to peer, to report,
To drunken sailor in the port,
To guard, to janitor, for safety from evil,
To dog of janitor, to keep his barking civil.

Free-form translated from Alexander
Griboyedov's "Disaster from Being Too
Smart" (1824)

Nobody cares about you, but you do

There was once a man called Trusty Bone. It happened that he fell in the chief's sight during a particularly bad moment. The tribe was hungry and the chief ordered them to eat Trusty Bone.

"You cannot do that to me," he cried. "I should not resist," he thought. "If I resist, they will have a reason to eat me, but if I don't, I am still one of them. They will not eat one of their own, they care about their own!" Then they tied his hands and threw him near the fireplace.

"Chief will change his mind; it's wrong and he cares about everybody," thought Trusty Bone, but the chief did not change his mind. "Our shaman will interfere, eating me will disturb the spirits of the tribe, and he will not permit that." But the shaman did not interfere. "My friends will get me out," he then thought. But his friends knew better. "My family…" he hoped in vain, but luckily his family did not do so, for they could have shared his fate.

Later, the chief finished his dinner and told one of his men, "Once somebody tried to do that to me…"

"And how did it turn out?" the man asked.

"That's how I became a chief," he answered.

You see, nobody cares about you. Well, your own kin–your family–may care, but they cannot help you. Everybody else just does not care. You are the only one who is responsible for your well-being–that is, for your mere existence. Nobody cares about you, but you do!

Are they really cannibals?

Many beginning cannibals start with this question. "Are these people around me really cannibals? It can't be true. They are so nice! No, really!"

The mythology of the island is full of stories about such non-cannibal tribes. They are kind, they are collaborative, and they don't eat each other. And most of the tribes pretend that they fall into this category. Would it be possible, by way of some weird accident, to land up in such a tribe, where everybody is a friend?

Let's try a scientific approach and consider what evidence we have to support the existence of such tribes in the present time. Most evidence belongs to one of two categories.

First, there are legends about the past. In this case, storytellers do not even try to pretend that past events happen now, so we can safely dismiss this category.

The second category describes the current place of a given witness's employment. In most cases, the tribe of the witness has a strong tradition of insisting that they are not cannibals. Renegades who dare to state otherwise are normally eaten.

Granted, most people don't look like cannibals. Moreover, they were not born as cannibals. With rare exceptions, men are not bloodthirsty, cynical, flesh-eating predators. And this is your chance, because you are neither. What makes them predators are the bare necessities of life: the need to feed their families, the need to save for retirement, the need to put their kids through college, and the need to pay their mortgages. Hey, you've got these needs too, don't you?

If you still have doubts, check for some signs of a cannibalistic tribe. Even if it pretends to be non-cannibalistic, it usually cannot resist revealing some such signs. Does your tribe regularly use such phrases as "let him go," "restructuring," "downsizing," "maybe you need to change a career," or "we've lost him"? Have you ever considered what these words really mean? What does it mean for a cannibal to change his career when there are only two careers possible, either as a cannibal or as a food? Do people periodically leave your tribe, their leaving celebrated with food and drinks? Sounds familiar?

And if you still think, "Maybe that's not true, maybe I can live in peace with everybody around me," then think about your next meal. M-m-m, juicy! That's how you will taste if you are wrong.

You cannot eat a problem

It's sad but true. In other, civilized places, people tend to complicate things and hide this truth behind a lot of explanations, excuses, and reasons, but it's just that simple. You want food. You want to eat food. If you've got food, you eat. If you've got a problem, you don't.

It's really that simple. You cannot eat a problem, you can only eat food. If you've got a problem, that's nobody's problem but yours. You either solve it and eat, or you don't solve it and don't eat.

Let's consider a lesson from the island's history. There was once a young hunter Eager Bone, who was son of the chief. He got this name because he was eager to prove himself. It happened that the tribe went through a bad time. The chief sent Eager Bone out to hunt and told him, "It's your chance to prove yourself. Do it, bring the food to the people, and they will hail you as the greatest hunter of the tribe. Remember, you must bring the food, for I promised that to the tribe."

Eager Bone went out to hunt, but a flood started. All the prey either left the place, or drowned and got carried away in the water. Eager Bone returned and told that to his father, the chief. The chief turned his back to him and said, "Floods don't count." And then the chief added, "I did not see you. This is your luckiest day, because I did not see you with your pathetic excuses. I promised the tribe that you would bring food. They don't care, if food would be something that you brought on your shoulders, or you. They need food and they will get it. When I see you, you must have the food for our tribe."

This was really the luckiest day in his life, because many would not have gotten another chance. He was lucky to be the chief's son. He went for a hunt again and he brought food back for the tribe.

You see, it's really that simple. In the end, problems don't count. You either have a problem or food. It's your choice.

> # Floods don't count.

That's not your tribe

Let me tell you a story. Smart Bone was an excellent hunter. He always knew where the food was and how to get it. With him the tribe prospered and never had to starve. He was like a blessing for the whole tribe, except for the tribal Chief Eating Officer, Bare Bone. As a tribal CEO, Bare Bone had to direct the tribe, and it often happened that Bare Bone was pointing in one direction while Smart Bone preferred another. As you may have already guessed, Smart Bone was usually right, and Bare Bone was usually wrong.

Bare Bone was not a bad leader. He understood that Smart Bone provided an enormous value to the tribe. So he tried to talk to him. He explained to Smart Bone the value of the teamwork, playing along, and following the strategic directions given by him, Bare Bone.

"That's bullshit," Smart Bone said, "Are you telling me that I should lead my people to the wasteland just because you have chosen the wrong direction? How can I do that to them? They rely on me, and I should bring them to the food."

"Sometimes we have to go with the team, even if we don't agree with the team's decisions," explained Bare Bone patiently, "And sometimes, as a leader, you have to take responsibility for the team's actions, even if you don't agree with them."

"'Team' means you, right? Why should I follow you, if you are wrong? I should feed my tribe, not follow idiotic orders!" argued Smart Bone.

"I would recommend that you change your attitude towards teamwork," Bare Bone answered, "You see, this is really important to your work, and you cannot be successful without it. Are you sure that the career of a hunter is right for you?"

Guess what happened next? Right. Smart Bone was advised to change his career. With the help of a few of Bare Bone's assistants, he did so that same night. Not surprisingly, his new career was being food.

Remember, unless you are CEO, it's not your tribe. Of course it's nice when your tribe prospers, but it's stupid to risk everything so that the tribe prospers. If the tribe really cares, it will find a way to get your advice. If it does not, why bother? Especially if doing so is dangerous and has no chance of success?

Chief will always be able to turn everything his way, because he has the power, and you don't. Occasionally, you can fight the chief and win, but what's in it for you? A slightly more successful tribe? And the chances of winning are next to nothing. On the other hand, the chances of losing are very high, and you could lose everything without a second chance.

The next time management makes some stupid decision, try a simple exercise. Calm down, close your eyes, and tell yourself, "This is not my tribe!" And you will see how much simpler your life becomes.

"Give not that which is holy unto the dogs"

"Give not that which is holy unto the dogs,
neither cast ye your pearls before swine,
lest they trample them under their feet and
turn again and rend you."

Matt 7, 6

Never give people something they cannot appreciate. Even if their life depends on it. Let us recall the story of a greedy cannibal and his naive savior. There was once a cannibal, let's call him Greedy Bone. He was so greedy that whenever somebody extended his hand for a handshake, he thought they wanted him to bite it. Since there were few people who wanted to live without their hands, nobody was shaking hands with him.

Once Greedy Bone fell into the lake. He did not know how to swim, so he started to drown. People were standing on the land, but none gave him a hand to help him out of the water. None, but one, who cried, "What are you doing? He will drown!" Then he extended his hand to Greedy Bone, trying to pull him out of the water. Guess what Greedy Bone did? The same thing he always did–he bit it off, and then he drowned, because, well, he did not know how to swim.

You see, in order to rightfully give something, two conditions must be met:

1. The person must understand what it is you are giving to him, and why he needs it.

2. The person must really want it enough to be grateful if you give it to him.

In the case of Greedy Bone, none of these conditions were met, and you see how it ended. He could have been better off if he were given a wooden stick or something else that was hard and non-edible. That's of course–again–if he would appreciate its purpose. And his savior would have been much better off as well.

This rule applies in different shapes and forms, but essentially: you should never give others the best of you. It's dangerous, it's not worth it, and you already have yourself and your family to give the best of yourself.

Give not that which is holy unto the dogs; keep it for the ones who are holy to you.

But never hesitate to give some bullshit

That's true. Although giving something that is holy and dear to you away to another cannibal is wrong, giving per se is a necessary part of your existence. Some management gurus say that giving creates an atmosphere of abundance, which serves you first and then returns in real value. Less metaphysically, it simply means that to make people give up something to you, you first need to give up something to them.

The cheapest way to do this is to give something that is worthless or almost worthless to you. Be aware, however, that you should never downplay the importance of what you give. People often value things not by their actual value, but by the value they see others apply. If you are a giver, don't hesitate to show that you perceive real value in the thing you're giving. Otherwise, how would the takers realize that they owe you now?

You should also be careful. If others start identifying you as somebody who gives mostly bullshit, that may be very bad for you. You'd rather give some bullshit that others care about. Such bullshit is easy to find if you know where to look. After all, everything in the world belongs to one of three categories. There is that which is holy. There is food, which is what being a cannibal is all about. Then there is everything else, which in the end is just bullshit. And that's a lot. Create an atmosphere of abundance around you–give some of it to others!

Beware of a shaman

A shaman is the high priest of your tribe. Depending on your tribal beliefs, he could be a witch doctor, a priest, a prophet, a fuehrer, an architect, a visionary, or simply a highly paid expert. Whatever is the name, the essence is the same. This is the person who "communicates" with higher powers, whether they are personified forces of nature or the latest "State of the Art Scientific Truth."

In any case, it's something you have no control over, and something that the shaman presumably represents. This is what makes him dangerous. Everybody thinks that he is just a messenger. Killing a messenger will not help you to prevent anything he is warning you about. It does not matter that his warnings and threats are complete bullshit, because everybody believes that they are not.

A shaman can scare people away from you. He can compromise people's willingness to follow you. He can even make people hunt you as food. And you cannot do much to fight him, because people are afraid of the powers he represents. It does not help that these powers are completely imaginary and never really existed in the first place. And even if they do exist, your shaman usually has no clue of what they want or how to contact them. These powers are not what's threatening you. Your people, who believe the shaman, are the threat.

The power of a shaman has two bases: "higher powers" nobody can control and nobody (including the shaman), can really understand, and the people, who believe that the shaman represents these powers. Even if you don't care about "powers," you still need people, and if they believe in something you're opposed to, you cannot do much about it. But what can you do to protect yourself? Surprisingly, you can do quite a bit.

First, as a passive defense, be nice and friendly to the shaman. Ideally, get him on your side. A shaman can be a threat, but he can be your greatest ally as well. Put a bit of these "powers" behind your throne, and everybody trying to steal the throne automatically becomes a tyrant, an usurper, and an ignorant fool, who will bring the tribe to a certain doom. Not bad, huh? And don't make a mistake: as much as you need the shaman, the shaman still needs you. If you play it right, the shaman will bring you success that you would never achieve alone.

Second, if possible, have several other shamans backing you up. Therefore, in a case where one of them turns his back on you, you will be able to rely on the others to neutralize the betrayer.

Try to balance their power, so that you always will be their arbitrator. Balancing their power generally means that you want the weakest to get stronger, and the strongest to get weaker. What is even more important than balancing, though, is trying to support the ones who support you.

Getting the weakest stronger is relatively easy. You just need to say here and there that "this new guy really knows..." or something like that. However, there are a few things to be careful about when you do that. Do not threaten other shamans. Be sure this new shaman is backing you up. And don't "over-inflate" him until he becomes the strongest, because then you will need to counteract that.

Getting the strongest weaker is trickier. You can push up all the others, but this approach has certain limits. You don't want to push their collective power to levels where they won't care about you.

Just blaming the shaman for something does not work. The logic of higher powers, whatever they are, is always the same. When something is going well, the powers should be credited for the success, but when something goes bad, real people are the problem. Especially those real people who don't believe in powers or, even worse, blame the shaman for the failure. Don't become that person.

One interesting way to get somebody down is to praise him to the wrong people. You can praise a dangerous shaman to somebody with power who does not like you. Or you can falsely put the praise in the mouth of a person who is never trusted, and whose approval is the worst curse a manager or a politician could imagine. See below in "Beware of omega."

The third thing you can do is get some shaman powers for yourself. It does not matter what the powers are, as long as some people, especially people in power, believe in them. Go talk to some ancestor's spirits in a forest, or start to use Object-Oriented Design and Six Sigma quality initiative, or get your tribe ISO 9000 certified. Anything will do, as long as your chiefs believe that it does. Be careful, however, in devoting too much of your time to such things. Being a full-time shaman is a lifetime commitment without an easy way back.

Beware of shamans, and keep in mind that sometimes you cannot do anything about them, especially when the shamans become holy cows.

Beware of a holy cow

A holy cow is a different beast. It usually does not have direct power to harm you, but that does not mean that you can consider it food. In fact, doing so may be very foolish, because holy cows are protected, and they sometimes have indirect power to fight back.

Consider the wife of your chief; the old man whose presence is considered a lucky charm for the whole tribe; the old buddy of the shaman; or the tribe's chief advisor. These are evident cases. But sometimes they're not so evident. How do you know that somebody is a friend of a shaman or a chief? Or worse, how do you know that their wives are not friends?

Holy cows are different, but they have one thing in common: they are well-protected by either the strongest members of a tribe or by the whole tribe. Holy cows don't attack by themselves, but they can be extremely destructive. They often can do terrible things to anybody, including the whole tribe, and suffer no consequences because of their protection.

Let's suppose a trusted chief's advisor says that a group of hunters should go to the mountains because they will find a good hunt. So the best hunters go up there and become food for a neighboring tribe. Who will be blamed for this? The advisor? No way. The hunters! The advisor gave them perfectly sound advice, but they were simply not able to use it. Sounds familiar?

We never said that logic has any value in tribal affairs, and actually, we are repeating the opposite throughout this book. In cases where holy cows are involved, logic is especially harmful to those who dare use it. When they are involved, everybody uses a different kind logic: the holy cow is right, and everybody who does not agree with him is wrong. Facts don't matter, you don't matter, the whole tribe doesn't matter, and the past and future don't matter, either. If a holy cow said one thing yesterday and a completely different thing today, then the world had simply changed in the meantime.

Don't argue with a holy cow. Don't get in the way of a holy cow. If a holy cow is in your way, find another way. Because otherwise, you are stepping into cows' greatest specialty: bullshit.

Beware of an omega

Cannibalistic tribes tend to suppress the human nature of their members. It's no surprise that, as a result, they show the signs of animal social behavior. In particular, they become in many ways similar to rat packs. In fact, a lot of the advice in this book can be easily illustrated using animal social behavior models.

In a rat pack, there is a minimal number, sometimes just one, of alphas or alpha-males. An alpha is the rat king, something very similar to the chief of a tribe. He is allowed everything and he gets most of the food, and nobody else can do anything about it.

An alpha is surrounded by betas, who suppress any opposition to the alpha and to themselves. Betas also hope to become alphas one day, which makes the alphas keep an eye on them. If an alpha thinks that some beta has become too strong, powerful, or influential, he can terrorize, set other betas against, or kill him. Occasionally, some beta becomes too strong and powerful. In this case, he challenges the alpha and, if he succeeds, he becomes the new alpha.

All these games occur on top of the mass of suppressed gammas, who actually bring the food to the pack. Gammas are the ones from whom the food is taken.

There are many more gammas than there are betas or alphas, so if all the gammas decided to attack, the betas and alphas wouldn't have a chance. For this reason, betas cannot physically suppress all the gammas at the same time. It's done more by an example. And omegas are the example. So named for the last letter of the Greek alphabet, they are the last in the pack. They can be terrorized or killed at will, even by gammas. In fact, gammas are encouraged to do so by betas and alphas, because it gives them a bit of "beta" feel, and at the same time warns them about the consequences of disobedience.

Throughout history, omegas have had various names: outcasts, untouchables, Dalit, scapegoats, lumpen-proletariat, people scum, and a lot of others. Notice that slaves are not omegas; they are gammas or, you could say, "deltas."

You don't want to be an omega. An omega is basically food waiting for a dinner requiring extra meat. No decent cannibal would want to be even close to becoming an omega. However, because of their terminal position, omegas often carry amazing destructive power. Moreover, though hunting omegas is normal social behavior, it does not bring you any points, and it may often be as dangerous as hunting down gammas or even betas. Let's see what tends to happen:

Scenario One: Scapegoat

The name of this scenario explains its essence. Imagine that some alpha screwed up, and we mean a major screw-up. For example, he started a Great Strategic Thinking Initiative and stuffed it with a bunch of morons.

To start with, morons are known to produce hectic activity without any visible reasons or benefits for those involved. That makes the entire tribe hate such an initiative, and somebody then has to be held responsible for causing the hatred. In the next step, the morons are going to give their Strategic Directions. Then the tribe will have to do something about it. If the chief rejects their ideas, something will have to be done with the morons who suggested it, but they can be useful the next time. If the chief accepts it, somebody should be responsible for the consequences.

The common solution is very simple. The chief puts some omega in charge of the morons. If somebody has to be responsible for the unfortunate results, that's the omega, who is used as a scapegoat. And if everything goes well, the chief gets the credit, because who would credit an omega for success? In the latter case, as a reward, the omega may be spared until the next time.

Apparently, such an omega has to be kept around until his time comes. Therefore, assaulting such an omega before he met his fate may not be quite welcome by the chief or the betas. At the same time, an omega among morons has a lot of opportunities to blackmouth everybody he does not like. And you don't want to be that person.

Scenario Two: the Omega of a Fallen Beta (or Alpha)

Though omegas are often the ones to blame for their own problems, they are not the ones who appoint themselves as omegas. It's usually some beta or alpha who chooses some gamma and makes him an omega. Now, imagine that for some reason such a beta is not supported by other betas and alphas. Imagine that he falls out of favor and is going to become food.

How are these guys going to rationalize eating him? One way is to blame him for the unfair treatment of some gamma, and then reinstate his omega as a gamma. Then everybody who hunted the newly rehabilitated omega is a prime candidate to become food, too. You need to know with whom you should hunt, and with whom you should not.

Scenario Three: Revolutionary Omega

This scenario never happens in rat packs, but it's known to happen quite often in human societies. Some omegas occasionally fight back, get support from gammas, and end up as new alphas and betas. Old alphas and betas become food in the process. The smaller the group is, the more likely this is to occur. And tribes are usually pretty small groups.

Beware of revolutionary omegas, don't cross their paths, and keep an eye on them. That's especially important if they are backed up by some higher-level alpha. Sometimes aligning with a revolutionary omega, though risky, may bring you to betas and even alphas faster than you ever could have hoped. There are a lot of alphas who reached their positions in exactly this way.

Scenario Four: Spot the Hunter

Alphas encourage betas–and they together encourage gammas–to hunt omegas. However, you get nothing by doing so. The only thing these hunters get is an alpha-beta feeling of themselves. For many, this is an ample reason. But this exposes you as somebody that is trying to excel. Gamma who wants to become beta. Beta who wants to become alpha. That is, a *competitor*. Got the idea?

Scenario Five: Omega Has Nothing to Lose but Becoming Food

Omegas have nothing to lose. You do. Whatever he does will not affect his future, because his future is mostly predefined. But it can affect yours. See the point? Look at the advice, "Be nice to a janitor's dog," and you will understand that an omega is better left as it is. Hunted by others, not by you.

Join the praise

It's normally not good to join in a hunt for an omega. However, praising the already praised gamma is a completely different matter. Being a cannibal is a lot like being a teenager in high school, competing head-to-head with others for popularity. You gain popularity by associating with more popular folk (alphas and betas); you lose popularity by associating yourself with losers (omega.)

Some people think that they can gain popularity by avoiding conflicts with alphas and betas, and by hunting omegas. While they are right on the first assumption, the second part has serious defects, as discussed above.

Praise, on the other hand, is a completely different beast. You can practice praise in public or in private (which are different things as well).

By praising a person in private, you are improving your chances that the person will not hunt you, even if he will gain power. It's called building a relationship. Don't hesitate to praise anybody in private, even a hunted omega. Hunters will not know you praised him, and in the event that the victim and the hunters trade places, you'll have an ally.

The only case when you need to be moderate with praising in private is when the person is a complete loser who is sucking the lifeblood and luck out of everybody he is associated with. We all know such walking disasters, and the farther you keep from them, the better.

Public praise associates you with the person and with his group, including anybody who has praised the person before. That may be beneficial or it may be disastrous. If you publicly praise a hunted omega, you associate yourself with him. Need more explanations as to what that means to you?

Such is a reason why you should be careful with public praise. After all, today's beta may be tomorrow's omega. However, there is one case when it's as safe as it can be among cannibals. If some person is regularly praised by your chief, the chief of your chief, and the chief of this person, you'd better join in and praise this person for something too. You see, teenagers in schools have to go for popularity to determine their alphas and betas, but you don't. Your alpha is your chief, and the chief of your chief. No doubts, no problems. By praising somebody he praises, you are associating yourself with him.

A word of caution is due, however. If your tribe happens to be more intellectual than the average tribe, you'd better avoid just repeating the boss's praise. Unless, of course, he likes that kind of stuff. It's usually better to find another reason and another time for that. You can also do it without that person or your chief around. It does not hurt if they are present, but association works in the heads of listeners, and when delivered indirectly it is often more efficient.

Don't befriend others,
they could be your breakfast tomorrow

Of course, we are not talking about having fun together. Sharing a glass or two of coconut beer never hurt anybody. What hurts is long-term loyalty.

Frankly, in our experience, there is no such thing as long-term loyalty at all. People either don't have it, or they become food too soon for their loyalty to become long-term. There is one important exception. Every cannibal should have unsurpassed, eternal, and unquestionable loyalty to himself and to his family. But this is the only exception.

Imagine that you've got a friend, and the chief said that he is food. What can you do? Your loyalty will require protecting him. But then you will become food as well. So, what's the point? Even if you don't fight for your friend, but you refuse to take part in his demise, that's no good. You will set yourself apart from the conformant crowd, and this is not something your chief will ever forget.

But maybe loyalty to your chief is appropriate? Think again. What if you've got a new chief? Should you preserve your loyalty to the previous one? Do you really think that's a good idea? If yes, what will you get? The answer is not encouraging. At best you will get nothing. At worst you will alienate your new boss and may even become food.

So whatever you do, loyalty hurts.

Be nice to a janitor's dog.

Be nice to everybody: to your boss, to your peers, to your reports, to your partners and customers, to total strangers, to all kinds of small people around you, like the helpdesk specialist, the janitor, and the janitor's dog, just in case. That does not mean you have to waste a lot of time on them, not at all. Just be nice. Why? It's pretty clear about your boss, and kind of clear in terms of peers and partners, but why the janitor's dog?

Make a simple comparison. What will the dog lose if it becomes food? Life, of course, but what is his life? Is it a lice-ridden sleeping rag, being beaten by its master, and a Sunday bone?

You see, the dog can bite you because it has too little to lose, and it's likely been beaten to the point where it does not care about the future. But you do. So beware.

But what if it cannot bite you for any number of reasons—whether it's your current position or dog-proof pants or even some secret weapon? Think now: why do you believe it cannot bite you? Are you sure about this? Do you really know everything?

Many beginning cannibals wonder why they should be nice to everybody when the chief of their tribe is not. In fact, he is rude, arrogant, and lazy. So why? Does his example prove that this advice is useless? Not at all. Do you know how your chief was acting when he was not a chief yet? Are you sure he got there by not being nice? As to what he is doing now, isn't it better to think about it, when you become a chief yourself?

> # Be nice to a janitor's dog.

Never write a nasty memo, eat it, or leave it

If a cannibal from another department was rude to you, never be rude back. Be polite. Be especially polite when you eat him (remember, fork goes to the left hand). Be even more polite if you leave him for later, because now he gets a chance to eat you first. Don't forget to apologize before eating him. It costs you nothing, but he will taste better.

Remember, a message carved in stone exists for a very long time. One of the main goals every decent cannibal should pursue is to remain a cannibal and not become food. A nasty memo carved in stone stays around and gives others a formal reason to see you as food. You don't want that to happen.

Smile, show your teeth!

"Smile, darn you, smile!"
(song from "Who Framed Roger Rabbit?")

Smile! Don't just show a smile, really feel it. Smile from the heart. Some people think that you need to be happy to smile. Wrong! It works the other way around. You feel happy when smiling.

You need more reasons to smile?

- A smile makes others to like you.
- A smile shows that you are strong and self-confident.
- A smile shows that you are well fed and not hunting right now.
- A smile relieves you from stress.
- A smile attracts the opposite sex.
- A smile releases endorphins in your body, which make you feel happy.
- A smile improves your digestion.
- A smile prolongs your life.
- A smile costs nothing.

Got it?

Make your enemy love you

If you are already a good cannibal, you know that everybody is an enemy except yourself and your family. But some enemies may be more dangerous than the others, so they will require more attention.

The trick is to make them emotionally attached to you, to make them need and enjoy your presence. And if they irrationally believe that you can improve their future, that doesn't hurt either. Notice "believe," though.

We don't assume that you will really improve their future. After all, you have more important things to do.

Ideally, you may be able to induce long-term loyalty from others, and that's good. As it was described before, long-term loyalty is something you need to avoid, because it leaves a cannibal at a disadvantage. And you want others at a disadvantage, don't you?

Is this a bit too cynical even for a cannibal? Yes, maybe. But why do you care?

And finally, should you love your enemies? Yes, definitely. It just should be a different kind of love. And for that, you need to know how to cook them properly.

Make your food enjoy being eaten

Yes, this is possible and quite beneficial. For starters, it just tastes better and is much more healthy. Vegetarians believe that when food is screaming in fear, it fills itself with hormones of fear and panic. Therefore, when you consume it later, you also consume these hormones, imposing the stress of extra fear upon yourself. Even without hormones, screaming and fighting food spoils the appetite and may be just plain dangerous.

This leads us directly to the second reason why this is really important. It's not so often that a person is eaten in a single act. It's usually started by reducing somebody in status, getting him lower and lower, and only eventually eating him. During this time, it is much better if you maintain good relations with your future food. This way, your food is more submissive to what you are doing. It really believes there is some good about the things happening around. It enjoys every day and it may actually help you reduce it to food. Can you think of a better way to make food out of somebody?

If you think bigger, you will see the third evident reason why making your food enjoy the process is important. What if you don't succeed in eating this person? What if he recovers and maybe even gets some power? What if he leaves the tribe and becomes the chief of a new one? What if you need to seek shelter in his tribe in the future? If you made him enjoy the process, you have nothing to fear. Keep this in mind. True cannibals always do.

You may think that it's easy to advise, but not very easy to follow. To some extent this is true. However, if you take a look around, you'll be surprised by how many people enjoy being eaten. Here are some sentences that you may use to smooth the digestion process:

- We need to do the right thing!
- Let's see how we can optimize the process.
- I really believe you would be just great in this new role!
- Good thinking, man! It's a really smart move on your side.
- Yeah, who wants to be stuck in the same role forever?

Give respect, get respect

Many cannibals misunderstand this phrase. In fact, they understand it as a reciprocal thing, so when they don't get respect, they don't feel obligated to give respect. That's absolutely wrong.

Even though the two parts of this rule sound similar, they are completely different concepts with completely different purposes. And missing one part does not mean that you can ignore another one.

So what does it mean to give respect? Actually, it means a lot of things. To start with, never be rude. Do not offend others. Why would you? Does being rude accomplish anything positive for you? Yes, the person will feel offended, but can you eat it? No, even a good offense is not a food. In fact, an offended person is often harder to eat than one who trusts you. So why would you do that?

The second aspect of giving respect is to listen to others. We already mentioned the great chief Bare Bone. Once, his tribe was hungry again. People grumbled at the lack of food, and some blamed Bare Bone for it. There was one man in the tribe, named Ugly Bone, who was known for his quarrelsome and disrespectful behavior. When the tribe met to discuss their problems, Ugly Bone stepped forward and said, "You are a very bad chief! The tribe relied on you and you betrayed us. We are hungry, and we have nothing to fill our bellies! Are you a leader or what? Let me tell you: you can eat me, but you will never be a good leader for our people!"

"Yes, we'll eat you, Ugly Bone. Thank you for such a generous offer!" answered Bare Bone. The tribe ate that day and Bare Bone was forever remembered as a savior of his people.

You see what happened? Bare Bone gave respect to Ugly Bone. He listened to him, even though Ugly Bone was rude. And he did not just listen to him. He actually implemented Ugly Bone's idea. And who is remembered now as a savior and a leader? Right, Bare Bone. You see, ideas are cheap unless they are implemented. And the one who actually implements an idea gets the real credit.

To be a leader, you must do. You can think, but as has been demonstrated by numerous leaders throughout history, that's not a requirement. In fact, the leaders with the lowest IQs are often the most remembered and revered. So listening does not hurt. Somebody really can come up with a good idea, something better than you have. So what? You implement it, and you get the credit!

This brings us to another aspect of giving respect–giving credit. Does it contradict what we said few lines above? Not at all. Consider the example above one more time. Bare Bone implemented Ugly Bone's idea, and he did not forget to credit it to the author. Did this hurt him? No way. He actually benefited from giving the credit. Ugly Bone became a selfless hero who gave his life for his people. And Bare Bone became a savior by implementing the solution. Notice that he became savior, not a ruthless cannibal. You see, this a clear win-win situation, a masterpiece of Bare Bone's art of management.

Now about getting respect. Because giving respect is your responsibility, you may think that somebody else should give you respect, while you can rest. Wrong! You need to be as active in getting respect as in giving it. In fact, you need to be even more active. Getting respect for yourself is your responsibility. Getting respect is taking respect.

The true meaning of win-win negotiations

In older times, negotiations were always considered to be "win-lose." That means that if one side wins, another side loses. Or, simply put, "win or lose." This led to unreasonable confrontation and a major waste of resources, when such was not necessary at all. The major breakthrough occurred a relatively short time ago, when a "win-win" approach was discovered. Since that time, the "win-win" approach became a major style of negotiation, and you must learn it to become a successful cannibal.

Let's start with the story of how "win-win" negotiations were invented.

Once, two cannibals were traveling with their tribe's shaman. They were his honorable bodyguards and companions. They wondered into a deserted area that was deprived of food. Not surprisingly, all the food supplies were reserved for the shaman, leaving these two guys very hungry.

One night, the lack of food resulted in a violent fight, which could only end with one cannibal becoming food for the other. This was a typical old times "win-lose" negotiation, that could not end well. At least it could not end well for one side (and not very well for the other, for that manner). The incident ended peacefully, though, when the shaman woke up and gently advised his companions to put their differences aside.

Later, both cannibals prepared to sleep, wishing to recover from both the fight and the shaman's gentle advice. They started to talk.

"If the shaman hadn't interfered–" the first cannibal started.

"Then you would have been my food," the second cannibal continued.

"Huh! If only the shaman was dead–" answered the first cannibal.

"If he was dead–" started the second one, and that was the moment of Truth.

"–we would have enough food and we would not have to fight!" the second cannibal finished.

You've probably already guessed what happened next. The opponents joined forces, killed the shaman, and had enough food to get out of the deserted area and safely return home. They used the win-win approach on many later occasions and became living legends and leaders to their people.

You see, there is a certain benefit in replacing win-lose negotiations with win-win negotiations. To be clear: win-win simply means win-win-lose, which is when two negotiators join their forces and resources to make somebody else lose. Then they share the loot and they are both winning.

Win-win-lose negotiation is a very powerful tool; every modern cannibal should be aware of it and skillful in applying it to everyday situations. Win-win negotiations can provide you with the necessary leverage against your old enemies and rivals.

Granted, a lot of times you negotiate with your enemies and rivals. But for every single enemy you negotiate with, there are a lot of enemies you can get rid of–if you apply the win-win strategy. And if some of your enemies apply the same strategy, you will be able to successfully resist their attempts to eat you. That's something you cannot achieve alone.

Does this mean that the cannibal you negotiated with becomes your "friend"? Not at all! He will eat you at his earliest convenience, and so should you! The only problem is that you are on the same boat and you need each other. That means that the "earliest convenience" will not come soon, or may not come at all. But that does not matter in a principle picture, for he is still your enemy and your potential food. It's also true the other way around.

So be alert, be careful, and know when win-win negotiations have to be replaced with the "win-finally lose" kind. Be especially alert if you suspect your "partner" has decided that it could be feeding time.

In a black and white picture people tend to become confused about colors

Not just colorful colors like red, blue, yellow, or green. People are also getting confused about what is black and what is white. Not to mention what is good and what is bad.

Surprising, is it not? However, it's true. Imagine a picture. Yellow sun, blue tropical sea, green grass, gray stones…Does this help you? No, absolutely not! Beautiful as it is, that's just a bunch of facts. That's not judgment!

Now, envision the same picture in black and white. White sun, light sea, dark grass, black stones…You see? There is just one step required for making judgments. Good sun, good sea, bad grass, bad stones. You see? It's that easy.

And it does not matter which one you call good, and which one you call evil. Just read again: bad sun, bad sea, good grass, good stones. Does it raise any protest in you? No. And there is a very good reason as to why. Because this good-evil contrast did not make any sense in the first place! The sun is not evil, but it's not good, either; it's just a bright sun. Similarly, the sea, the grass, and the stones are not good or evil, they are just the sea, the grass, and the stones. But because of their colors, you can make some ridiculous associations, which nobody will question you about. And then, because they are already ridiculous, there will be no problem when it comes to inverting them, should you wish to do so.

In a color picture, everything stays just as it is. It does not have to move anywhere. Blue is just blue, and red is just red. But in a black and white picture, people need to move everything to one of two extremes–into either the white or the black. The world becomes so simple to them that they are trying to maintain this simplicity at all costs. "If you are not a friend, you are an enemy." "If you are not with us, you are against us!" How many more such proverbs can you recall? Probably quite enough.

So how do you benefit from that? The secret is in the definition. Who is good? Who is a friend? Who is with us? And who are "us"? Do you know who? You are! A color contrast picture is a perfect way to get people on your side. And it does not matter if you are really good. In a black and white picture, people will be too confused to see the difference.

Never underestimate people

Never underestimate people's capacity for screw-ups, stupidity, misunderstandings, unproductive grudges, ignorance, and other great traits which set us apart from the animals. If you say something, check that they understand. If you ask somebody to do something, check that it gets done. Or better, first ensure that they understand what you're asking.

Let's consider this with an example. Two young brothers, Hungry Bone and Yummy Bone, lived together in a cave that they got from their parents.

Their parents had not proved themselves to be good cannibals during one hungry winter, when the brothers were too small to hold culinary interests, but that is a completely different story. Hungry Bone became a successful hunter, while Yummy Bone took care of the cave and attended to social issues. They lived in a very uncannibal-like way between two of them, taking care of each other, protecting each other, and fighting together through life.

They became increasingly strong and influential within the tribe. One time, Hungry Bone was invited to the tribe council while there happened to be no food in the cave. So he told his brother to get some meat for dinner.

When he returned home, there was no meat, but a pile of rotten tomatoes in front of the cave's entrance. "Where is the meat?" Hungry Bone asked his brother.

"You know, I thought that we could use a good steak sauce, as you like it," Yummy Bone answered. "But there was no one around, so before going for the meat, I decided to get a sauce. I was not able to get any, but I found these tomatoes that I could make some with. And I'll tell you, that was not easy."

"But they are rotten!" protested Hungry Bone.

"That's okay; we are not going to eat them fresh. We will make a sauce for the meat," explained his brother.

"And have you got the meat?"

"Nah," answered Yummy Bone. "I had no time for that."

What's the moral of this story? Of course, the number one rule is never be angry at your family. But the second one is that even the best people can screw up.

Don't forget: you plan on becoming the Chief Cannibal, your tribe's Chief Eating Officer, right? That supposedly means that you are the best. So, the others are not.

After all, if you spent half your life trying to become smarter than the rest of the tribe, why complain that you are surrounded by idiots? Yes, you are smarter; that's what you have worked so hard for. And now you have to live with that.

No last words

Sometimes good advice is appropriate. Sometimes the truth may be appropriate. In your life in the tribe, you may develop unnatural affiliations with some other cannibals, which almost reminds you of friendship. Actually, you may really develop a friendship, at which point both advice and truth may be appropriate.

However, never forget that true advice and truth are holy. See the section "Give not that which is holy unto the dogs." If somebody whom you count as a friend betrays you, that's your mistake. That's your huge mistake. Don't make it even bigger by giving departure gifts of advice or words from your heart. Don't give last words of friendship. There is no departure from a friendship. You just never were in one.

And next time be careful about selecting your friends. Or better yet: be careful now.

People say that a friend would never betray you if you don't have a friend. But there is more to it than that. True friends don't betray. False friends never betray, if you don't have false friends.

In public, talk much but tell nothing

Public speaking is tricky. When there are a lot of people around you, each one of your words can be understood in a lot of ways. You can also receive a lot of different reactions to each single word. Most barbarian tribes on the island tend to express such reactions by throwing flowers or stones at the given speaker. Even if your tribe does not, this model will vividly display what we are talking about. When you talk tête-à-tête you can fence off a single stone. Can you fence off a hundred?

However, like it or not, you have to speak in public. And you want as much flowers, and as little stones, as possible. Many beginners think that their speech has just one single dimension: what they say. Based on this assumption, they are trying to say things that will make some stones be replaced by flowers. What they don't understand is that in a big enough crowd they will still attract enough stones to be stoned to death (or, at least political death).

See for yourself. Suppose you make a speech in front of 90 people, and two out of every three cannibals in the audience will throw something your way. That's 60 cannibals. If half of them like you and the other half don't, that's 30 stones. If you win over half of your opponents, it's still 15 stones. Too bad.

Now, let's see where beginners make a mistake. There is actually another dimension in any public speech. This dimension reflects how many people are interested in throwing anything at all. Suppose that in the same speech you did not achieve any shift in power, but 90 percent of your audience did not have an emotional response leading them to throw something at you. That means that only 10 cannibals threw something at you, and with a 50-50 breakdown, that's just 5 stones. Much better, right?

It's like a control with two knobs on it. One determines the proportion between flowers and stones, and another determines how much will be thrown overall. The first knob helps, but the second one saves.

How can this be done practically? People throw things when they get emotional. They don't get emotional when you simply talk. On the contrary, your posture, apparent self-respect, and visible optimism can make them more comfortable and quiet. That's what you want. Besides, you want them to see you—to see you talking, and to see your posture, self-respect, and optimism. That makes them feel that they know you, and that you are important.

People get emotional when you say something that really interests them. For example, how many of them will soon become food, or which of them will become food. In the second case, you will definitely get a lot of stones. You see? Talking is safe, but actually telling something is not.

Talking without telling is a high art. Did you ever wonder why the chiefs of large tribes never make any sense? Did you ever ask yourself the same question about the chief of your own tribe? That's because they've mastered the art of talking without telling. And you need to, too.

In most cases, not telling is easy. Replacing your message with self-important but incomprehensible mumbo-jumbo is what requires hard work. Try to repeat the words of your tribe's chief in front of a mirror. Even better, repeat his words with self-respect and visible dignity in front of your fellow tribesmen. They will not dare to make fun of the chief's words, and you will get some invaluable training.

Try simple sentences first. For example:

Sentence to train	Translation to avoid
"The food resources utilization factor in our tribe substantially grew compared to the same quarter of previous year."	We ate more people in our tribe.
"The strategic mission of our tribe is to provide substantial improvement in a food supply for a targeted cannibal population!"	Only a few left; everybody else is tagged as a food and eaten.
"Last year, strategic restructuring of resources allowed us to substantially cut costs and become a more slim, energetic, and efficient tribe."	Neighboring tribe captured and ate half of our people.

Suppose you still have to actually tell something. There are many techniques for this case, as well. First of all, you may choose some omega to do so. You can even give him to the crowd afterward. A little feast is always very good for managing disturbed public emotions.

Another way is to represent your message in a most optimistic manner. This is also a high art, but you can master it with sufficient training. Consider, for example, how a master would say these phrases:

- We are much better now about not wasting any food.

- I want every decent cannibal to have enough food.

- In these tough times, I am proud of you, people!

Never show a weakness

There is a poker saying that goes, "Never let them see you sweat." What does weakness mean among cannibals? It shows that you are food. It shows that you are easy food. What else? That your family is easy food, too. In especially bad cases, it also shows how to make you food.

What good comes from showing your weakness? Alas, nothing!

Never show a weakness.

Don't trust, Don't fear, Don't beg

This is probably the main rule of survival in a tribe of cannibals. It's actually a quote. One great omega of the past[1] stated it as a survival rule for every omega. However, it's a great rule for every cannibal, even alphas. No alpha should trust anybody around, because they all want to be in his

---

[1] Actually, it was said by Alexander Solzhenitsyn about survival in concentration camps.

place. No alpha should ever really fear. That would show his weakness, and it would signal others that it's time to take over. And no alpha should ever beg. If he can, he should take; if he cannot take, begging for something will not get him anything. But anyway, you are not alpha, you are most likely gamma, maybe beta, or, God save, omega. So why is this rule so great for you?

First, you cannot trust anyone. They are cannibals, and you are food to any cannibal. Can you trust anybody who sees you as food? Not likely. This does not mean that you cannot expect them to do what you want. You just have to ensure that they see it as something good for themselves, that they really plan to do it, and that they won't screw it up. You can deal with them, you just cannot trust them. You are the only one you can really trust.

Of course, there is always your family. They don't consider you food. Or at least you should hope not. But family is usually not really a part of the tribe.

Second, you should not fear. Fear is a primitive emotion. An evolved brain does not have much use for primitive emotions. Fear, and then anger, helped our ancestors to survive in the African savanna by first trying to run away and then, if that did not help, by fighting. Unfortunately, our own kind is much more dangerous and cunning than African predators, so these simple emotions are usually just another enemy you have to face. Fear makes us run away, but there is nowhere to flee within a tribe. Anger makes us fight, and it may be useful as your last chance before being cooked. At all other times, you don't face a physical fight, because when it comes to that, it's usually already too late (if it comes to that at all). And what's the use of adrenaline pumping in your blood? The troubles of evolved men are much more complex and thus require much more complex responses. And complex responses require cool heads and clear minds.

Notice that the absence of fear does not mean the absence of caution. More caution is often better than less caution. Some may call caution fear, but don't let them confuse you. There is a difference between a thoughtless flight from trouble and a calculated evasion of trouble. Too many have tried to prove the absence of fear by inviting trouble onto themselves, and only those who evade trouble are around to tell their stories.

Now about the third part of this rule. Don't beg. There are no free lunches among cannibals. Trading is of course different. Favors are also different, because ultimately they are merely a form of trading. Trading is okay as long as your partner cannot freely escape leaving his part unfulfilled.

Begging is useless and damaging. It cannot achieve its objective because you have nothing to offer in return. And the other person is a cannibal; he does not care about you and he does not care about your needs, or even your survival. Why would he give something up for you? And even if he does, you still show your weakness and give him a way to control you. Such a thing is too dangerous to let happen among cannibals.

Don't trust, Don't fear, Don't beg

YOUR JOB

*Make others do for you whatever they love
to do, and you will not have to work a
single day for the rest of your life.*

Bare Bone

Know your business

Let's start with a story. Faithful Bone was a Fire Keeper. In his time, peo-ple did not know how to create fire. So they had to keep it on all the time. If a tribe lost the fire, tribesmen had a miserable life until the next forest fire, because they could not warm themselves up, they could not cook food, and they had no protection from wild animals. Faithful Bone was the best Fire Keeper in the history. For all time he was on duty, the tribe never lost their fire. When bad times came, the tribe slowly ate members of Faithful Bone's family, but he still kept the fire going. And the very last thing he did—before he himself was eaten—was prepare more fuel for the fire in which he was cooked. His last words were, "I'm just doing my job."

Faithful Bone became a legend, but frankly, do you want to be like him? He thought that his job was to keep the fire, and maybe he was right. But what did he get for doing his job? His family was eaten and he did not avoid the same fate. Why? Because he did not know his business.

The business of every decent cannibal is attaining food for himself and his family. Can you carry your business by just doing your job? If so, you are the lucky one. But most likely, you can't.

Remember, you and your family are the ends, and your job is just the means. And unless you have the ends, they cannot justify the means.

Know your job

Knowing your business does not mean that you can neglect your job. Your job and your business are just two sides of the same coin: the coin of your success. Your business is your strategy, and your job is your tactics. Strategically, you want to provide for your family, live long, and prosper. Or, in other words, to become the Chief Eating Officer of your or any other tribe. Tactically, you can achieve it in many ways, but most of them are essentially the same. You have to serve the ones who are (at the moment) higher than you in the food pyramid. And that can only be done by knowing your job.

An alternative way is to create your own tribe. But then you need to know your job even better, because the fate of your new tribe will depend on it. After all, in such a case the success of your tribe is the whole point of the exercise, right?

Okay, suppose you agree that you should know your job—but what is your job? Some would say that's easy to answer, for there is a job description. But in fact, it's a very tricky question. Let's return to the story of Faithful Bone and his demise.

The fire in his tribe was considered a mystical gift from above. Therefore, traditionally, fire keepers in his tribe reported to the shaman. Times were very bad for the tribe, and people started to growl at the shaman. Why? Because when things start to go bad, and people cannot understand why, they look for reasons beyond their understanding. And who in the tribe is responsible for reasoning beyond the understanding of a normal cannibal? The tribe's shaman.

As usually happens in such cases, the shaman told them that the people called the trouble upon themselves by following a bad leader, the tribe's Chief Eating Officer. To prove that, the shaman needed a very good sign from above or, even better, several signs from above. One of them would be a loss of fire. Being a very serious tragedy to the tribe, a loss of fire was always attributed to forces beyond people's comprehension. With all this in mind, the shaman said at the tribe's meeting, "Our ancestors will take fire from the tribe to show they're angry at our Chief!"

Faithful Bone was at this meeting. Only a person both deaf and stupid would not get the shaman's message. Faithful Bone was not deaf, but he clearly was stupid. He said, "Let the forces beyond do their job, and I will do mine!" And he did. The tribe did not lose their fire. We know what happened next.

You may think that Faithful Bone still did a very good thing. He sacrificed himself and his whole family, but he kept the fire going for the tribe. But you would be wrong. Faithful Bone's successor was not deaf. The next day he lost the fire. The tribe suffered greatly, the chief was eaten, the shaman strengthened his powers, and everything proceeded according to plan—with only one difference, without Faithful Bone and his family.

The cleverest readers are likely to wonder what happened to Faithful Bone's successor? And they would be onto something because, by the law of the tribe, the fire keeper who lost fire had to be eaten. And he was. Now you may wonder, what could he have done about it?

Once, I was a fire keeper in the same position as Faithful Bone and his successor. I was neither deaf nor stupid. I deserted to another tribe. And I still think that this was the best answer to that question. Because any other answer would likely be the same one that Faithful Bone got. I just decided to mind my own business. After all, business is strategy and jobs are just tactics, remember?

Stay on the stuff jobs, not staff jobs

Stuff jobs are all about the stuff. They give food to the tribe. That includes raids on neighboring villages, spotting potential food sources inside the tribe, and even spotting the slaves who cannot be used efficiently anymore. These jobs pay with the better parts and the stable flow of food.

Staff jobs–like sharpening stone axes and supporting the fire–are essential for the life of the tribe, but they don't pay. You are getting whatever was left after the stuff (a.k.a. line) jobs. You are at the mercy of the food providers. You are easy to replace, and you are therefore worthless to the tribe. So, you are likely to be targeted as the next food if things go south.

Always take a job that brings more food

After all, that's why you are working. There are other reasons as well. First, the more food your job brings, the more the tribe respects you. It's a sign of your status. The more food you get now, the more food you will get in the future.

Don't let yourself be lured by funny titles and vague promises of future prospects. Suppose that you have to choose between a 15 percent raise (and your next raise will also be 15 percent), or you can settle on 5 percent for now, but the next time, if everything goes right, maybe you'll get 30 percent. Now stop and think for a minute. If you give up the 15 percent raise for 5 percent now, what are the chances that you will be offered 30 percent next time? Or is it more likely that you'll get 5 percent again with more promises?

There is another side to this as well. Consider a job that gives an abundance of food, and another job that gives barely enough to survive, or even less. Guess where you would have to work more? If you answered "first" or "second," you are wrong. The right answer is both! Yes, when you negotiate, you only negotiate what you will get out of the job. Whether you will get a lot or almost nothing, you always offer the same effort from your end. And they will get it from you.

Whether you wash dirty skewers after tribal meals or lead the tribe in a war, you will still get to your hut, cave, cabin, apartment, single-family residence, or palace in the same pitiful condition, washed up, squeezed like a lemon, and barely recovering for your next day at work. That's what you negotiated for. It's simple: if you negotiated for almost nothing, then nothing is what you get for your life. And if you got a lot, at least you have something to show for the wasted years of your life. Makes sense?

The easiest career path is to become a food

Life is not easy. Be ready for that. After all, the easiest thing is to become a food. Do you want that? No. Avoiding that fate is not easy. You can play defensively by trying not to become food without trying to make others into food, or offensively by taking the option of eating you off the table by eating any potential offenders first. In real life, you can never use one of these tactics alone; it will always be a mix of offensive and defensive tactics.

The proper balance is often dictated by circumstances and environment rather than by your preferences. But whatever the case, both tactics are not easy. All you can do is brace for an impact and push on through.

This may all sound trivial, but there is more to the story than just that. If you belong to a large and sophisticated tribe, you have definitely heard about career paths. It's also likely that you were asked which path you prefer. It normally comes down to one of two choices: managerial or individual contributor. The thing is, though, in the end there are just two true career paths—cannibal or food. Strictly speaking "an individual contributor" is not necessarily food. Shamans are often individual contributors, and most shamans are quite decent cannibals. But unless you can become a shaman, the individual contributor role means being a food.

It is no accident that this path is more readily available. After all, becoming food *is* the easiest career path.

Have fun doing your job

First of all, what is your job about? It's about eating others. Can you have fun while hunting and eating your prey? You'd better. Because you are either a hunter or prey, and I've never met people who are having fun while being hunted and eaten.

Hungry and angry are not the traits of a successful cannibal. In fact, if he is hungry, he is a terribly lousy cannibal, isn't he?

And besides, everybody likes happy and smiling people. For some irrational reason, some people may like you even while you are eating them. They are, of course, clearly mental cases, for one should not like anybody who tries to eat him, whether the eater smiles or not. However, the fact is that some people do just that.

Even if they don't like you when you eat them, they get less opportunities to get help from other cannibals. Why? Because other cannibals will be more sympathetic to you. They will think, "Hey, this guy smiles, he is happy, he even tries to be nice to this shouting idiot, he has to eat. How could he do something wrong?"

And the last (but not the least) reason is your own health. A cannibal's life is not easy. In fact, there is a lot of stress in every day of your life. There is practically no way to take a vacation from the cannibal business. If you do get out of the tribe for some time, you will need to pick it up later or give up something. How do you survive such stress? Like it or not, there is only one way. The way is to take it lightly, have fun, and really enjoy all this stuff going around you.

If you don't, you may want to think about a career other than being a cannibal. Even though there is only one career other than being a cannibal. That is being food. It's your choice.

The only way to improve the multiplication table is by making it wrong

Think about it. There are things that are so basic and evident that you simply cannot improve them. There is only one multiplication table. 2 x 2 is always 4. If it's 5, that means there was an error in calculations, nothing more, nothing less.

Well, a naïve person, generally referred to in this book as food, would say that this means only one thing: you don't try to change unchangeable things, like physical laws or arithmetical rules, but rather use them to your advantage. In a lot of cases, that's true.

However, a true cannibal has another use for such laws. Let's get to the story.

When the famous chief Bare Bone was not yet a chief, but was close to becoming one, he faced an unpleasant problem. Many members of the tribe did not trust him and were willing to challenge his leadership and authority. He would never be the greatest cannibal in history if he could not resolve this little problem, which he did.

Once, at a tribal meeting, he suggested an interesting solution to the problem of feeding the whole tribe.

"What is our problem?" asked Bare Bone, who answered himself, "Not having enough food. But why don't we have enough food? It's very simple. Our hunters are just too lousy with arithmetic. When they get two members of a competing river dale tribe on one day and two more on another day, they bring just four of them. They think that two plus two is four, so that's what they bring. That's nonsense! If they would improve their arithmetic and make two and two equal five or more, they could bring over five, six, or even seven members of that river dale tribe! What we need are hunters who are better with the arithmetic!"

So, what do you think happened next? The non-compliant hunters, who were always challenging Bare Bone's authority, started to complain that it could not be done because two and two is always four. Others understood that they needed to capture five or six enemies every two days. So they became the hunters who mastered the new arithmetic, and the ones who were not eaten.

You see, the very unchangeable nature of such laws makes them perfect tests of conformity and loyalty. Such tests help you weed out those members of the tribe who are non-compliant and have the guts to stand against you. And they give you an excuse to eat them.

Don't take your job home

Your job is being a cannibal. That calls for successfully eating people and not letting yourself be eaten. Who are the people around you at home? Do you really want to eat them? Wouldn't that defeat the very purpose of being a cannibal? After all, the reason you have to be a cannibal is the need to provide for your family, right?

It's also very important because doing your job well is an all-consuming task. You have to be so deep into what you are doing that it almost makes you a different person. This person you've become should be a very effi-cient cannibal. However, this person cannot really live in a family. Cannibals don't have any loyalty other than to themselves. When out-siders lose, you eat. In a family, it's different. When anybody in your fam-ily loses, you lose. Being involved with your work at home brings that ruthless person into your home. You don't want to see such a person in your home, and nobody in your family wants to, either.

There is another side to this story as well. Being a cannibal is very stressful. Can you really maintain the tension 24/7/365? Maintain it for too long and, whether you are a good cannibal or not, it will not matter. You'll die of natural causes: stress and exhaustion.

YOUR CHIEF (BOSS)

#1. The boss is always right.
#2. If the boss is wrong, see #1.

Folklore

Don't think like CEO,
know what your CEO thinks

Some gurus recommend that you think like your Chief Eating Officer. The assumption is that if you think the same way a successful and respectable person does, then you too will be successful and respectable. That's awfully wrong.

To start with, the whole argument is based on the assumption that CEOs *think*. Yeah…Think again. That simply is not necessarily true. We know a lot of brilliant and successful chiefs who made history purely on dumb luck, without the slightest clue of what made them so successful.

Even if some CEO does think, that does not mean that's what made him a chief. There are a lot of other factors that must be credited for his success. How about eating competitors before they became competitors? Or what about brown-nosing before he became CEO? And what about all the other advice given in this book? If you've noticed, a lot of it has nothing to do with *thinking*.

Some people also misinterpret such advice. They try to think like they are already CEOs. Ouch…Not much can hurt more. Think about your current CEO. Who is he? Do you think that he is an all-wise all-powerful visionary, attentive to his people's opinion? If so, good for you. But the chances are that he is just a know-it-all who-the-heck-you-are always-right jerk. Do you want such a person on *your* team? Why do you think your boss will be excited to see you acting this way? Hint: he will not. Seriously.

To think and to act like a CEO does not help. To understand what your CEO thinks does help. This is what you actually should be doing. If you really know what your CEO thinks, you can get ahead, suggesting ideas he favors, and avoiding ideas he does not.

Though it's easy to say, it's not easy to do. First, you need to think like you are in his place, but not too deep. Then, you have to subtract the right ideas which he would never be able to come up with. Then you have to guess the wrong ideas he will inevitably hit along the way because of his personal flaws. You cannot perfect these three steps using science. It's more of an art.

You need to keep in mind all three steps at the same time. In short, you should not think like a CEO, you should think like *your* CEO. See the difference? You need to miss the same opportunities and fall for the same mistakes as he does. And then, use this knowledge to become his champion.

Can you give him a great idea or prevent him from falling on his face? Yes, you can, but it will not help you much. See below about that.

Of course, this does not only apply to your CEO, it applies to all of your bosses, including your direct boss.

It does not matter
if your chief is right or wrong...

Imagine that your chief has decided that the Earth is a sphere[2]. You know that Earth is flat, but should you try to prove him wrong? Faith is a very

---

[2] The islanders are not very keen with geography. However, on the contrary to the common belief, most of them don't believe that the Earth is flat. Most of them just don't care.

strong thing. Belief is a weak form of faith, and as such it's also relatively strong. If you tell your boss that the Earth is flat, what would you achieve? He will think that you are wrong. He will also think that maybe you are not that useful, so it could be time to use you as food. That's it.

Now imagine that you think the Earth is a sphere, and your chief thinks it's flat. What happens when you tell him your point of view? Guess what? He will decide that you are wrong! You see, it's exactly the same thing. No difference whatsoever.

So for you, there is really no difference if your chief is right or wrong. What matters is what he **believes** to be right. If you can change what he believes, that may matter, too. But the point is that whether it's right or wrong does not matter at all. It may be the greatest bullshit, but if you can sell it, you are in. The sale matters; being right does not.

It does not matter
if you are right or wrong either

Consider the last example thoroughly, and you'll see that it does not matter if you are right or wrong either. Again, if you can make your chief believe that you are right and others are wrong, it matters. It's not necessarily a good thing, but it matters.

In any case, the important thing is what your chief believes and whether or not it coincides with what you are saying. So why shouldn't you pass on the middleman of your opinion and say directly what your chief believes?

Some inexperienced cannibals think that it's simpler to make your chief change his opinion if you are right. Think again. First of all, changing something is always more complex than leaving it as is. Yes, occasionally it may be beneficial to change your chief's opinion, but it does not matter if you change it to right or wrong. And it's important to first evaluate if the benefit is worth the trouble. Also, in many cases your chief may become jealous and annoyed by your cleverness. So the actual effect may be negative.

The Boss is always right.

No kidding.

Bring your Chief good news

Everybody loves good news. If you have some, bring it to your chief first. If he likes to hear good news (and believe me, he does!) he will want you around to share more. That's both opportunity and insurance. It's an opportunity to be around the chief, to learn from him, to eat some food from his table, and to eventually take his place. It's an insurance that nobody will consider you food, because nobody wants to argue with the chief, and he likes you.

This is not so hard; just tell him all the important good news that he would like to hear. If you need to, make sure good things happen, and then be the first to tell him. If necessary, push other people to make it happen, and then tell him. If absolutely necessary, tell him, and then push other people to make it happen! Attribute the results mostly to yourself; because after all, do you want to promote yourself or somebody else?

Occasionally you can share a piece of glory with somebody who is essential to your success. But be careful. Remember, if you are to be the only two cannibals left, he must be the food, not you!

Bring your Chief bad news

This is a bit trickier. Nobody likes bad news. But...nobody likes even worse news either. So if you have bad news, bring it early, not later. The crucial thing is the approach. Imagine a cannibal who approaches the chief saying, "Chief, the dam is going to break soon. We will all become food! I missed the moment when it started to break down. I am sorry, chief! I am food!" The only decent thing the chief can do is agree with you, "Yes, you are food." Do you want that? Probably not.

Now consider another approach. "Chief, I found that the dam is damaged. Let me take strong cannibals to fix it. If we fail to do so, we may become food, and I can prevent it right now!" See the difference? Now you are the savior. You see, instead of reporting doom, you bring good news. The dam may be fixed. The tribe is safe! This is actually an example of the old rule: "Always make a solution out of a problem."

By bringing bad news in time, when you can still fix it, you replace a problem with a solution, and preserve the role of a good messenger. And if you are too late, well, it will not matter anymore. Your whole tribe, including you, is food anyway.

A word of caution is due, however. Be careful with this approach. The bad news should be evidently bad news. The chief should not think that you are asking for something unimportant–and some chiefs will. What do you do then? Well, you will have to wait until the danger eats the chief, and then you can try to fix the situation *as the new chief*. Fair enough?

Never ever threaten your boss

Your boss has to be a cannibal. You may want him as food, but he's a very dangerous food. In fact, he can use you as food almost whenever he wants to. So if the boss is dangerous, then the threatened boss is extremely dangerous. It does not matter if you never even intended to threaten him. If he perceives you as a threat, you are most likely going to become food.

You may expect a story here, but unfortunately, all the stories on this subject are too short, and they all boil down to a simple choice: "eat or be eaten." This happens throughout the island with the regularity of a well-oiled machine. When somebody intently or accidentally threatens his boss, he is eaten pretty soon. The boss may eat you yourself, give you to your peers, or even present you to another chief. The result will be the same.

This seems to be obvious, but we are not talking about you going to your boss and saying, "You are my food!" That would be really stupid. Your boss may feel threatened by much more subtle, and visibly unrelated, messages, which you may send without even knowing it. Let's consider a few statements that may be understood as threats:

> "I am your best hunter! Without me, your group will starve."
>
> "I am the only one in the group who can do that for you."
>
> "I must be rewarded with more food."
>
> "You cannot eat me. You need me!"
>
> "You are wrong. [And I am right!]"
>
> "You are so wrong. You cannot eat me."

Bottom line: any demonstration of your superiority to your boss, public perception that you are a more efficient cannibal than your boss, or mere indication that he may be unable to eat you, can be perceived as a threat.

In fact, some cannibals successfully use this to eliminate their most dangerous peers. They create a public fuss about the victim's superiority until the boss feels threatened and eats him. And even if you fail, the dangerous peer is so flattered by your brown-nosing that he could be okay for you to be around for some time.

By the way, from all of this, you should now have a pretty good idea of what to do if you are a threatened boss. *Bon appetite!*

Don't travel with the Chief or the Shaman

Traveling with a chief or a shaman is bad. You have to do whatever they do and you cannot use the extra time to learn or relax. They see you all the time, and they may notice something you don't want them to notice. And you know, there is *a lot* you don't want them to notice. Remember, you are their potential food!

What's even more dangerous is that you are spare food. You went to the peace negotiations of a neighboring tribe? Guess who will be on the table for the feast? Imagine that you've gone to the wrong place, where there is no food. Guess who goes to the cauldron first?

That's not to say that you should never do so. Sometimes you just don't have any options. You cannot disobey a direct order, at least not in most cases. Or there could be a huge benefit in doing so. Just make sure this is a benefit for *you*, not anybody else, and make sure this benefit is ***real***. You know you can make a "Thank You" plaque yourself. It's not worth the risk of being eaten.

LEADERSHIP

Unless you are a lead dog, the scenery never changes.

Folklore

Be a lead rat

You need to be a lead. You need to be a rat.

If you put your time and resources into following somebody, you are playing with the things that don't normally exist in a cannibal world, like gratitude and fairness. Once the group reaches the goal, who gets the credit? The leader, right? Does he have any reasons to share the credit and benefits with the followers? Not many.

You may think that a smart leader would share the credit in the hope that his followers will stand with him through the next challenge. Think again. The life of a cannibal is short, and the time of association with a particular tribe may be even shorter. Your loyal cannibals may leave the tribe for reasons completely beyond your control, not to mention get eaten or reduced to omegas, who are basically walking food. With new ones, you would have to start everything again. Maybe smart cannibal leaders manage to handle that, but most cannibal leaders just grab all they can.

If you are a follower, how can you tell? The answer is that you cannot. So you will exist assuming something. If you are a leader, it does not matter while reaching for the goal. Your followers will act upon their assumptions. After you reached the goal, it does not matter either, because you already reached the goal. And for the next goal it will not matter if you have different followers. Be a lead. Be a rat. Be a lead rat.

Be a lead rat

Be physically fit

Hunters are slim and strong; food is fat. Be a hunter, be slim, and always be strong. That's pretty much the essence of cannibal wisdom. Imagine two cannibals, one slim and one fat, who both are spotted as potential food. Who do you think is more attractive as a food? Exactly–the fat one! Of course, if you are tall and strong and look like a mountain of muscles, you are very attractive as food, too. But!—If you are this strong, then you can decide who the food is. See the difference?

This goes beyond simple physical appearances. Your management strength reflects your influence on your chief, shamans, and peers. Your management body mass is the people you lead. They can be your muscle, or they can be your fat. To qualify as your muscle, they have to believe in you, and they have to do something important for the tribe, for themselves, and, most importantly, for you. They should put their own influence behind you. They need to be strong and they need to support you. As your muscle, they give you more influence and the ability to choose others as food. If they are fat, they are likely to be eaten by some other tribal manager.

Lead, follow, or get out of the way

Unless you have a very good reason to fight for something, these are your only options. What's behind them?

Let's start with getting out of the way. There are a lot of situations where you will choose this option. Simply put, this applies to everything you don't care about or just don't have the time or resources for. Everybody does that. Those who don't, quickly become food. Why? Because they just pick too many battles and they cannot put enough resources into winning any of them.

So for those things you choose to care about, there are only two options to choose from: lead or follow. Each of these options has pros and cons.

Following does not burn as much of your resources as leading does. It's always easier to follow an icebreaker than to be one. However, before following anybody, you need to be sure of three things:

1. What do you get by joining this leader?

2. Are the efforts of following worth what you are getting?

3. Are you a follower, or the rations?

For example, if your chief is "leading" something, it's worth it to join him as long as your participation is limited to showing support, and if you don't actually do anything (so you cannot be blamed for failure).

Be aware that following does not always come cheap. Are you sure that you will just follow an icebreaker, and not be used as an icebreaker? By following, you commit some resources to the cause and to the person. It takes great skill to join the winners without actually being committed to them or paying a price in resources. Unless you happen to be skilled at doing so, it's best to follow only if the price is not high or if you have no other options.

Unless these conditions are met, you'd be better off putting your resources somewhere else. See "Be a lead rat."

People are your greatest asset

Once there was a tribe that was torn apart by three brothers. The eldest brother took the best land and a lot of loyal followers, whom he could use as food at any time. He also got most of the food reserves. After he and his men left for greener pastures, the middle brother, with his own followers, grabbed the tools, weapons, and the rest of the food reserves, and occupied the second best part of the tribal land. He also did not want any real cannibals who were capable of competing with him. Instead, he took with him his loyal followers, who could fight for him but who would also submit to him as food.

This left the youngest brother in quite a complicated position. He found himself in a desert with no tools, weapons, or food, surrounded by hungry cannibals who would not submit themselves as food, but rather make food out of anybody that was unlucky enough to cross their paths.

However, a little time passed, and the tribe was again united under one of the brothers.

Guess which of the three brothers survived and became the chief? The youngest one!

The people of the eldest brother had quickly consumed the food that they got for themselves. As a result, they were stuck with no option but to slowly consume their own kin. You may think that good land provides enough opportunities to raise food, but cannibals are not very good at this kind of work. Besides, the ones who are good at raising food often become food themselves. So in no time, the eldest brother ate most of his people and was left with a few starving followers.

The middle brother's people found themselves in the same predicament, but with less food and more tools with which to kill each other. After a short time, an accidental stone from a slingshot killed the middle brother, and the rest of his people became a handful of hungry men without a leader.

During the same time, the youngest brother's people made tools and weapons that allowed them to hunt for people from the other two tribes. Why? First, because they could do that. They were the toughest cannibals, and they scared the elder brothers. They knew how to hunt. Second, they had no other options. They were all tough cannibals, and they knew how to stand up for themselves. So eating each other was not an option. The youngest brother looked like a tasty bit at first, but they knew that after eating him, they would have to fight each other. And they knew that they could not do that. That gave the youngest brother enough time to learn from his people and become the toughest cannibal around, so that nobody could eat him.

After a short time, the youngest brother's men conquered the rest of the tribe and made the youngest brother the chief.

You see? The eldest brother had land and the middle brother had tools, but they both failed. Why? Because they did not have the main thing that the youngest brother had. The people.

No knife fights by itself, no land produces food by itself (at least not enough food), and no tool works by itself. It's the people who fight, work, and produce food. And not just people, but good people. If you have good people, you have everything else. If you don't have good people, you have nothing.

You need to have good people, you need to make them follow you, and you need to make them support you. That's it. In the end it does not matter if you can do anything else or if you have anything else. Your people can and your people will get the missing pieces.

It's all about the people

Winners never quit, quitters never win

What makes a winner win? Of course, there is luck and circumstances. Of course, it does not hurt to be smart and educated. However, the most important aspect of a winning personality is persistence. When a loser begins a task, his record shows something like:

Fail, fail, fail, fail, fail, give up, lose.

For a winning person it's more like:

Fail, fail, succeed, WIN!

Of course, if you are eaten, you cannot try again. However, if you don't try, you will definitely be eaten. See the difference? If you continue to try, you may still be unable to win. However, you still have a fighting chance. And if you give it your best shot, you have a better chance. If you don't even try, you don't have a chance at all. Do you see any choice here?

Keep your men hungry (motivated)

A hungry man is an angry man, says folklore. That's true, but a hungry man is also a motivated man. Motivation may be positive or negative. There are three basic things that motivate a person: self-preservation, food, and procreation. Self-preservation motivates as a fear of death. It's nearly always a negative motivation. Procreation has mostly positive motivation, and it is beyond your control. Food is a unique motivator. It's both positive and negative, it affects everybody, and it spans into two other primary motivators. The lack of food threatens the very existence of a person, while extra food allows a person to feed his family.

It's very important to keep your men fed enough to survive, but no more fed than that. In this case, negative motivation prevents them from fleeing, and even small amounts of extra food provide a great motivation for putting extra effort into the job.

The same picture shows the dangers of overfeeding your people. A hungry man has two great motivators; an overfed man has only one. When they meet, the most motivated wins.

For your own sake and for the sake of your people: keep your men motivated.

Be a giving (feeding) hand

People like those who give them stuff. People like those who give them food. People like free cheese, even if it is in a mousetrap. People like those who set mousetraps with free cheese in them. Actually, you don't even need a mousetrap. After all, you don't hunt for mice, you want to trap people. And if they like you, they are trapped better than any mousetrap could ever do.

Why do you want people to like you? They are more likely to support you. They are more likely to follow you. They are less likely to eat you. And last but not least, they don't expect you to eat them.

However, a legitimate question is: where do you get the food? And if you share the food, do you have less for yourself? Not necessarily. There are many answers to the question of where to get food, and often giving brings you more food than you would get otherwise.

Let's recall history. Once, before he become the chief of the tribe, Bare Bone had an opponent. Big Bone was a hunter—strong, big, and skillful. Big Bone never liked Bare Bone, and the feeling was mutual. Not surprisingly, Big Bone wanted to eat Bare Bone. Nobody had any doubt that the first chance he got, Big Bone would satisfy his desire and Bare Bone would become food. In an honest one-to-one fight, Bare Bone had no chance against Big Bone.

However, things turned out differently. The tribe got bad luck and starved. At a tribe meeting, Bare Bone inspired his fellow cannibals and gave them food. The food was Big Bone, and he was big enough to feed the whole tribe, including Bare Bone. Just like Bare Bone had no chance against Big Bone, Big Bone had no chance against the whole tribe.

Would Bare Bone had gotten his share of food if he had not first given some to the tribe? No. He could not have handled Big Bone alone. You see, giving really pays. If you give, you get more in return. At least if you do it right.

Now you know the main answer. It's actually quite simple and logical. Where do you get the food to feed the people you want to feed? The ones who like you? With what do you feed them? With the people who don't like you!

This is just one answer to this question. If you look at the big picture, you can see many other ways to give your enemies to your friends. Giving their property, influence, and control over resources is an old and well-known way.

Let's consider resources. Does your tribe have a morale budget? It's likely that it does. Who controls it? Why? Have you ever thought about why this is so important? You've probably seen your chief pay for your whole team's dinner with the Tribal Platinum Card. Try to recall this moment. What feeling did it raise in you? Did it make you feel angry at your chief? Probably not. Even if you were angry at him before, after that he became "okay." Right? Such is the power of feeding your people.

As you can guess, the morale budget is something precious, which chiefs should try to get their hands on and jealously guard against competition. This is the food used to your advantage, and you should not let it be wasted to somebody else's advantage.

Imagine a tribe with 10 small chiefs and one big chief. Each small chief has just a few people reporting to him, and the big chief is the boss of everybody. The food in the morale budget is enough for each of the small chiefs to make several feasts for his people. Or, all this food can be thrown into one huge festivity organized by the big chief.

Now guess what the big chief will decide upon. Of course, a big party! A small feast will make people loyal to their small chiefs, because it looks like they are feeding the people. In the big celebration, the big chief is the central figure. That guarantees him all the credit that can be generated from the morale budget, and it helps him to keep the small chiefs under control.

Keep this in mind for when you become a big chief.

Mix and match people

You should apply this principle to both of the large categories of people that you deal with. It's true for people you lead, and it's especially true for the ones you eat.

One of the secrets of being a great cannibal chief is knowing how to form a hunting party. That means knowing how to form a team that can get along, avoid being eaten, and bring in food.

Let's consider an example. Imagine that two cannibals in your group are crazy about left ears. Then they become competitors. They both want the left ear of the next victim, and there is of course only one! Clearly, it's not the best idea to send them out together on a hunt.

On the other hand, if one of them wants the left ear, and another is crazy about the right ear, you have a perfect match. They will hunt food together as a team, because each of them will get what he wants.

This is not just about personal eating habits; you should match other personal preferences and skills. A cannibal who can track food and a cannibal who can kill it, are a good match. In contrast, two cannibals who are only good at tracking food may easily become food themselves. Another problem is if one of them likes male food, and another prefers female food. If they find multiple sets of tracks, they may lose valuable time arguing over which set to follow.

As for the people you eat, that's just common sense. You must eat a variety of food to be physically fit.

Be your own chief

Wherever you are, whatever you do, be your own chief. There is only one person in the world that you are really working for. That's you.

If some work does not make sense to you and does not benefit you, why do it? It may benefit your boss, your tribe, or the whole island, and that's really good. But first of all, it should benefit you. Otherwise, let somebody else do it.

You may argue that if it benefits your chief, he may be grateful to you. However, if he will be grateful to you, that will mean that the job benefits you, and then it makes a lot of sense. It's just that. It may directly benefit somebody else instead of you, but this "somebody" had better do something good for you.

In some cases, your choice may be about not doing something that's bad for you. Keeping out of harm's way is a legitimate goal. But you'd better get out of the tribe that only rewards a job well done by not punishing you.

Make yourself a chief

How do you think others became chief cannibals? Did somebody lead them to the top while holding their hands and advising them on each step? Or did somebody come up to them and say, "Starting tomorrow you are the chief"? Unlikely.

The truth is that you and only you can make yourself a chief. Others may help, if you are lucky, though most of time they will compete with you. And even if you are lucky, they still cannot make you a chief.

Remember, food is given, but power is taken. Nobody will give you the power unless you take it. That's what true leaders do. That's what you should do.

Leaders provide clarity

Yes, that's true. Whom will you eat today? Who is dangerous and who is not? What should a mere cannibal do to become a tribe's hero? And what should he not do to avoid becoming food? Your people look to you for leadership, and they look to you for answers to these questions.

There is another story about the legendary Chief Bare Bone. Once his tribe was caught without food for several days and people became ready to revolt. One of the tribesmen, Bone Dujur, asked the chief, "Where is our food? Are you chief or what? We need food for our families!"

Bare Bone asked the tribe, "Is he telling the truth? Do you want food now?"

The tribe, angry about their starvation and bad luck, cried, "Yes, we want food now!"

Bare Bone pointed to Bone Dujur and said, "He is your food!" The tribe was fed that day.

Did Bare Bone find food? Did he hunt for it? Did he lead his tribe to a place where they could find it? Eventually, yes, but that night, no. The only thing he provided to the tribe was clarity. "This is your food," he said. And so he kept his leadership and became the greatest chief of all time.

Clarity is one of the most valuable things to a cannibal. When you provide clarity, people follow you.

You cannot put a good man down,
just try your best.

Someone else got the job done, and you've got the credit? Somebody else has a good reason to think that you're a jackass, and he is vocal about it? Or, someone is just more qualified for the job you want? There are many cases when you have to get rid of someone.

There is a proverb that says, "You cannot put a good man down." So what? In many cases, whatever you *can* do to him is good enough. Say you manage to get him exiled into another tribe. Yes, he may be able to become their chief. But so what? He still cannot get you.

A word of caution is due here. What if in the future you have to seek shelter in that tribe? What if you will have to try to succeed there? Then it will be a problem. When you cannot reach an ultimate resolution, you need to take precautions. And as long as you have not achieved an ultimate resolution, you never know if you will be able to reach it, so you always need precautions. See "Make your food enjoy being eaten" for more about that. However, if you have a choice between being eaten and getting him out, which would you prefer?

Of course, eating him completely would be preferable, but if you cannot, settle for something "good enough." It really will be good enough.

(OMMON PIE(ES OF WISDOM

Put the people first

...and the dessert second.

All of being a chief cannibal is about self-confidence

...how else will others know that they should follow you?

Motivate and Energize Others

...whether at work, or in an oven.

Always make a solution out of a problem

...for example, a problem person may be great as food.

Have a lot of energy

…especially if you want a slow roast.

Prime on Execution: Deliver the Results

…a.k.a. food for yourself.

Have infectious enthusiasm about your job

…and don't forget to cook thoroughly, or you risk catching it yourself. Remember, heat processing kills bacteria. Get internal temperature to 165°F, 180°F if the poor thing was a chicken or a fellow rat.

Give and get

…never give without getting something back.

Go the extra mile

…or two, to ensure that they cannot catch you.

Don't manage, lead the pack

…after all, for a hunt you need wolves, or at least rats, not sheep.

Use your sense of humor

…see "Smile!"

Be careful with your sense of humor

…or somebody else will smile.

CONCISE CANNIBAL-AMERICAN DICTIONARY

Cannibal–that's either you, or whoever ate you.

Cauldron–salary fund.

Chief–boss, manager.

Chief Eating Officer–CEO, president, the big boss.

Eat–win over, neutralize, eliminate.

Feast[1]–a short period after performance review for the survivors.

Feast[2]–morale event.

Food[1]–money, wealth, power, benefits, bonus, other perks.

Food[2]–a party that failed in a competition.

Hunt–teamwork.

Hunter–a member of a team.

Tribe–a group of people who are trying to get an advantage over other groups by working together, while maintaining a gastronomical point of view on each other. Also known as a team, corporation, company, organization, or political party.

CONCISE AMERICAN-CANNIBAL DICTIONARY

Career change–reclassification of an unsuccessful cannibal into successful food.

CEO–Chief Eating Officer.

Company, corporation–a tribe established by a few cannibals and built by recruiting others as food.

Reorg, reorganization–a hunt in which some alphas and betas eat other alphas and betas. Gammas are usually just reallocated between new patrons.

Team–a tribe. Sometimes a part of the tribe that either considers the rest of the tribe as food, is considered by the rest of the tribe as food, or both.

Team player–somebody that is either ready to submit himself as food (playing along) or capable of using the rest of the tribe as food (demonstrating leadership).

Teamwork–a stratification process in which the strongest members of the tribe convince the rest to submit voluntarily as food.

Performance review–the process in which the lead cannibals remind the rest of the tribe that they are just potential food for the leaders.

Salary fund–tribal cauldron.

Vegetarian–a philosophy of motivating the food to stay at the bottom of the food chain.

Welcome aboard–an invitation to join the tribe. Depending on the circumstances, that's either behind the table or on the table.

BIBLIOGRAPHY

To become an even better cannibal you may want to read some of the books below:

1. 100+ Tactics for Office Politics by Casey Hawley-Barron's Educational Series, 2001, ISBN 0764116452, paperback, 184pp

2. 169 Ways to Score Points With Your Boss by Alan R. Schonberg, Robert L. Shook, Donna G. Estreicher, Donna Estreicher-NTC Publishing Group, 1998, ISBN 0809229994, paperback, 192pp

3. Big Shots, Business the Jack Welch Way: 10 Secrets of the World's Greatest Turnaround King by Stuart Crainer, Steve Crainer-John Wiley & Sons, ISBN 1841121517, paperback, 192pp

4. Buck Up, Suck Up...and Come Back When You Foul Up by James Carville, Paul Begala-Simon & Schuster, 2002, ISBN 0743224221, hardcover, 224pp.

5. Complete Idiot's Guide to Office Politics by Bob Rozakis, Rosemary Maniscalco-Penguin Group, 1998, ISBN 0028623975, paperback, 320pp

6. Control Your Destiny or Someone Else Will by Noel M. Tichy, Stratford Sherman-Harper Information, 2001, ISBN 1402876300, paperback, 684pp

7. Crucial Conversations: Tools for Talking When Stakes are High by Kerry Patterson, Joseph Grenny, Al Switzler, Ron McMillan-McGraw-Hill, 2002, ISBN 0071401946, paperback, 256pp.

8. Developing the Leader within You by John C. Maxwell-Thomas Nelson, 2001, ISBN 0785266666, hardcover, 224pp

9. Developing the Leaders around You: How to Help Others Reach Their Full Potential by John C. Maxwell-Thomas Nelson, 1995, ISBN 0840767471, hardcover, 192pp

10. Difficult Conversations: How to Discuss What Matters Most by Douglas F. Stone, Bruce Patton, Sheila Heen-Penguin Group, 2000, ISBN 014028852X, paperback, 272pp

11. Don't Send a Resume: And Other Contrarian Rules to Help Land a Great Job by Jeffrey J. Fox-Hyperion Press, 2001, ISBN 0786865962, hardcover, 172pp

12. Enlightened Office Politics: Understanding, Coping with, and Winning the Game-without Losing Your Soul by Michael Singer Dobson, Deborah Singer Dobson-AMACOM, 2001, ISBN 0814470653, paperback, 240pp

13. Execution: The Discipline of Getting Things Done by Larry Bossidy, Ram Charan-Crown Publishing Group, 2002, ISBN 0609610570, hardcover, 288pp

14. First, Break All the Rules: What the World's Greatest Managers Do Differently by Marcus Buckingham, Curt Coffman-Simon & Schuster, 1999, ISBN 0684852861, hardcover, 272pp.

15. Fish! A Remarkable Way to Boost Morale and Improve Results by Stephen C. Lundin, John Christensen, Harry Paul-Hyperion Press, 2000, ISBN 0786866020, hardcover, 112pp

16. Fish! Sticks: A Remarkable Way to Adapt to Changing Times and Keep Your Work Fresh by Stephen C. Lundin, John Christensen, Harry Paul-Hyperion, 2003, ISBN 0786868163, hardcover, 128pp

17. Fish! Tales: Real Life Stories to Help You Transform Your Workplace and Your Life by Stephen C. Lundin, John Christensen, Harry Paul, Philip Strand-Hyperion, 2002, ISBN 0786868686, hardcover, 128pp

18. Four Obsessions of an Extraordinary Executive: A Leadership Fable by Patrick M. Lencioni-John Wiley & Sons, 2000, ISBN 0787954039, hardcover, 183pp

19. Get Better or Get Beaten by Robert Slater-McGraw-Hill Companies, 2001, ISBN 0071373462, hardcover, 194pp

20. Getting Past No: Negotiating Your Way from Confrontation to Cooperation by William L. Ury-Bantam Books, 1993, ISBN 0553371312, trade paperback, 208pp

21. Getting Things Done: The Art of Stress-Free Productivity by David Allen-Viking Penguin, 2001, ISBN 0670899240, hardcover, 288pp

22. Getting to Yes: Negotiating Agreement Without Giving In, Second Edition by Roger Fisher, William L. Ury-Viking Penguin, 1991, ISBN 0140157352, trade paperback, 187pp

23. God Is My CEO by Larry S. Julian-Adams Media Corporation, 2002, ISBN 1580627641, paperback, 320pp

24. Heart of Change: Real Life Stories of how People Change Their Organizations by John P. Kotter, Dan S. Cohen-Harvard Business, 2002, ISBN 1578512549, hardcover, 208pp.

25. How to Become a Great Boss: The Rules for Getting and Keeping the Best Employees by Jeffrey J. Fox-Hyperion Press, 2002, ISBN 0786868236, hardcover, 176pp

26. How to Become a Rainmaker: The Rules for Getting and Keeping Customers and Clients by Jeffrey J. Fox-Hyperion Press, 2000, ISBN 0786865954, hardcover, 169pp

27. How to Become CEO: The Rules for Rising to the Top of Any Organization by Jeffrey J. Fox-Hyperion Press, 1998, ISBN 0786864370, hardcover, 162pp

28. How to Get Your Boss to Work for You by Faye Hardaway-PositiveWay, 1998, ISBN 0966266323, paperback, 310pp

29. How to Think like a CEO: The 22 Vital Traits You Need to Be the Person at the Top by D. A. Benton, Debra A. Benton-Warner Books, 1999, ISBN 0446673072, trade paperback, 480pp

30. How to Win Friends and Influence People by Dale Carnegie-Simon & Schuster, 1982, revised edition, ISBN 0671723650, mass market paperback, 276pp

31. It's Still the Economy, Stupid: George W. Bush, America's CEO by Paul Begala-Simon & Schuster, 2002, ISBN 0743246470, paperback, 208pp.

32. Jack Welch and the G.E. Way: Management Insights and Leadership Secrets of the Legendary CEO by Robert Slater, Vince

Lombardi-McGraw-Hill Companies, 1998, ISBN 0070581045, hardcover, 299pp

33. Jack Welch Lexicon of Leadership: Over 250 Terms, Concepts, Strategies and Initiatives of the Legendary Leader by Jeffrey A. Krames, Jack Welch-McGraw-Hill Companies, 2001, ISBN 0071381406, hardcover, 224pp

34. Jack Welch on Leadership: Executive Lessons from the Master CEO by James W. Robinson, Jack Welch-Crown Publishing Group, 2001, ISBN 0761535454, hardcover, 256pp

35. Jack Welch Speaks: Wisdom from the World's Greatest Business Leader by Janet C. Lowe-John Wiley & Sons, 2001, ISBN 0471413364, paperback, 256pp

36. Jack: Straight From the Gut by Jack Welch, Mike Barnicle, With John A. Byrne-Warner Books, 2001, ISBN 0446528382, hardcover, 496pp

37. Jesus CEO: Using Ancient Wisdom for Visionary Leadership by Laurie Beth Jones-Hyperion Press, 1996, ISBN 0786881267, paperback, 318pp

38. Leadership 101: What Every Leader Needs to Know by John C. Maxwell-Thomas Nelson, 2002, ISBN 0785264191, hardcover, 96pp

39. Leading Change by John P. Kotter-Harvard Business, 1996, ISBN 0875847471, hardcover, 187pp

40. Leading Change: The Argument for Values-Based Leadership by James O'Toole-Random House, 1996, ISBN 0345402545, paperback, 282pp

41. Making Horses Drink: How to Lead and Succeed in Business by Alexander Hiam-Entrepreneur Press, 2002, ISBN 1891984500, hardcover, 244pp

42. Managing Up!: 59 Ways to Build a Career-Advancing Relationship with Your Boss by Michael S. Dobson, Deborah Singer Dobson-AMACOM, 1999, ISBN 0814470424, paperback, 176pp

43. Managing Upward: Strategies for Succeeding With Your Boss by Patti Hathaway, Susan D. Schubert, Kay Keppler (Editor)-Crisp Pubns., 1992, ISBN 1560521317, paperback, 118pp

44. Managing with Power: Politics and Influence in Organizations by Jeffrey Pfeffer-Harvard Business School Publishing, 1994, ISBN 0875844405, paperback, 391pp

45. Never Work for a Jerk! by Patricia A. King-Watts Franklin, 1987, ISBN 0531155226, hardcover, 368pp

46. Never Wrestle with a Pig: And Ninety Other Ideas to Build Your Business and Career by Mark H. McCormack-Penguin Group, 2001 (Reissue), ISBN 0141002085, paperback, 304pp

47. Now, Discover Your Strengths: How to Develop Your Talents and Those of the People You Manage by Marcus Buckingham, Donald O. Clifton-Free Press, 2001, ISBN 0743201140, hardcover, 262pp.

48. One Minute Manager Meets the Monkey by Kenneth H. Blanchard, Ken Blanchard, William Oncken-William Morrow & Co, 1990, ISBN 0688103804, trade paperback, 137pp

49. Power Etiquette: What You Don't Know Can Kill Your Career by Dana May Casperson-AMACOM, 1999, ISBN 0814479987, paperback, 195pp

50. Power Etiquette: What You Don't Know Can Kill Your Career by Dana May Casperson-AMACOM, 1999, ISBN 0814479987, paperback, 195pp

51. Power of Focus: How to Hit Your Business, Personal and Financial Targets with Absolute Certainty by Jack L. Canfield, Mark Victor Hansen, Les Hewitt-Health Communications, 2000, ISBN 1558747524, paperback, 310pp

52. Primal Leadership: Realizing the Power of Emotional Intelligence by Daniel Goleman, Richard E. Boyatzis, Richard Boyatzis, Annie McKee-Harvard Business, 2002, ISBN 157851486X, hardcover, 352pp.

53. Richest Man in Babylon by George S. Clason-N A L, 2002 (Reissue), ISBN 0451205367, Mass Market Paperback, 160pp

54. Running with the Giants: What Old Testament Heroes Want You to Know about Life and Leadership by John C. Maxwell-Warner Books, 2002, ISBN 0446530697, hardcover, 112pp

55. Secret Handshake: Mastering the Politics of the Business Inner Circle by Kathleen Kelley Reardon-Doubleday & Company Inc., 2002, ISBN 0385495285, paperback, 272pp

56. Selling You! (2 Cassettes) by Napoleon Hill-St. Martin's Press, 1987, ISBN 0940687291, audio, 2 cassettes

57. Seven Habits Of Highly Effective People by Stephen R. Covey-Simon & Schuster, 1990, ISBN 0671708635, paperback, 319pp

58. Teamwork Makes the Dreamwork by John C. Maxwell-J. Countryman, 2002, ISBN 0849955084, hardcover, 120pp

59. The 17 Essential Qualities of a Team Player: Becoming the Kind of Person Every Team Wants by John C. Maxwell-Thomas Nelson, 2001, ISBN 0785274359, hardcover, 156pp

60. The 17 Indisputable Laws of Teamwork: Embrace Them and Empower Your Team by John C. Maxwell-Thomas Nelson, 2001, ISBN 0785274340, hardcover, 256pp

61. The 21 Indispensable Qualities of a Leader: Becoming the Person That People Want to Follow by John C. Maxwell-Thomas Nelson, 1999, ISBN 0785274405, hardcover, 157pp

62. The 21 Irrefutable Laws of Leadership: Follow Them and People Will Follow You by John C. Maxwell-Thomas Nelson, 1998, ISBN 0785274316, hardcover, 233pp

63. The 25 Sales Habits of Highly Successful Salespeople by Stephan Schiffman-Adams Media Corporation, 1994, ISBN 1558503919, paperback, 130pp

64. The 25 Sales Strategies by Stephan Schiffman-Adams Media Corporation, 1999, ISBN 1580621163, paperback, 128pp

65. The Book of Management Wisdom: Classic Writings by Legendary Managers by Peter Krass (Editor)-John Wiley & Sons, 2000, ISBN 1402893183, hardcover, 492pp

66. The Five Dysfunctions of a Team: A Leadership Fable by Patrick M. Lencioni-John Wiley & Sons, 2002, ISBN 0787960756, hardcover, 240pp

67. The Five Temptations of a CEO: A Leadership Fable by Patrick Lencioni-Jossey-Bass Inc., 1998, ISBN 0787944335, hardcover, 134pp

68. The GE Way Fieldbook: Jack Welch's Battle Plan for Corporate Revolution by Robert Slater-McGraw-Hill Companies, 2000, ISBN 0071354816, paperback, 288pp

69. The Mind of the CEO by Jeffrey E. Garten-Perseus Publishing, 2000, ISBN 1402885989, hardcover, 320pp

70. The New GE: How Jack Welch Revived an American Institution by Robert Slater, Jack Welch-McGraw-Hill Companies, 1992, ISBN 1556236700, hardcover, 295pp

71. The One Minute Manager by Kenneth H. Blanchard, Spencer Johnson-Berkley Publishing, 1983, ISBN 0425098478, paperback, 111pp

72. The Tipping Point: How Little Things Can Make a Big Difference by Malcolm Gladwell-Brown Little & Company, 2002, ISBN 0316346624, paperback, 304pp

73. The Zen of Groups: A Handbook for People Meeting with a Purpose by Dale Hunter, Anne Bailey, Bill Taylor-Perseus Publishing, 1995, ISBN 1402848676, paperback, 196pp

74. Think and Grow Rich by Napoleon Hill-Ballentine Publishing, 1976 (Reissue), ISBN 0449214923, Mass Market Paperback, 233pp

75. Throwing the Elephant: Zen and the Art of Managing Up by Stanley Bing-HarperCollins Publishers, 2002, ISBN 0060188618, hardcover, 240pp

76. Time Tactics of Very Successful People by B. Eugene Griessman-McGraw-Hill Companies, 1994, ISBN 1402877099, paperback, 240pp

77. Whale Done! The Power of Positive Relationships by Kenneth H. Blanchard, Jim Ballard, Chuck Thompkins, Thad Lacinak-Free Press, 2002, ISBN 074323538X, hardcover, 128pp

78. What Would Machiavelli Do? by Stanley Bing-Harper Information, 1999, ISBN 0066620112, hardcover, 176pp

79. When Smart People Work for Dumb Bosses: How to Survive in a Crazy and Dysfunctional Workplace by William Lundin,

Kathleen Lundin-McGraw-Hill Companies, 1999, ISBN 0071348085, paperback, 185pp

80. Winning Office Politics: Dubrin's New Guide for the '90s by Andrew J. DuBrin-Prentice Hall Press, 1990, ISBN 0139649581, paperback, 337pp

81. Winning Ways: 4 Secrets for Getting Great Results by Working Well with People by Dick Lyles, Richard I. Lyles-Penguin Putman, 2000, ISBN 140287961X, hardcover, 93pp

82. Work in Progress: Risking Failure, Surviving Success by Michael D. Eisner, Tony Schwartz-Hyperion Press, 1999, ISBN 0786885076, paperback, 450pp

83. Your Road Map for Success: You Can Get There from Here by John C. Maxwell-Thomas Nelson, 2002, ISBN 0785265961, hardcover, 244pp

0-595-28380-2

www.ingramcontent.com/pod-product-compliance
Lightning Source LLC
Chambersburg PA
CBHW030746180526
45163CB00003B/925